Radical Sports
ORIENTEERING

Neil Champion..........

www.heinemann.co.uk
Visit our website to find out more information about **Heinemann Library** books.

To order:
 Phone 44 (0) 1865 888066
 Send a fax to 44 (0) 1865 314091
Visit the Heinemann Bookshop at www.heinemann.co.uk to browse our catalogue and order online.

First published in Great Britain by Heinemann Library,
Halley Court, Jordan Hill, Oxford OX2 8EJ,
a division of Reed Educational and Professional
Publishing Ltd.

Heinemann is a registered trademark of Reed Educational
& Professional Publishing Limited.

OXFORD   MELBOURNE   AUCKLAND
JOHANNESBURG   BLANTYRE   GABORONE
IBADAN   PORTSMOUTH NH (USA)   CHICAGO

Designed by Celia Floyd
Originated by HBM Print Ltd., Singapore
Printed in Hong Kong by Wing King Tong

ISBN 0 431 03673 X (hardback)
04 03 02 01 00
10 9 8 7 6 5 4 3 2 1

ISBN 0 431 03682 9 (paperback)
04 03 02 01 00
10 9 8 7 6 5 4 3 2 1

British Library Cataloguing in Publication Data

Champion Neil
    Orienteering. – (Radical sports)
    1. Orienteering – Juvenile literature
    I. Title
    796.5'8

Acknowledgements

The Publishers would like to thank the following for
permission to reproduce photographs:

Cloud Nine, pp. 4, 6, 26-29; Gareth Boden, pp. 5, 8-25;
Robert Howard, p. 7; TVOC, p. 25.

Cover photograph reproduced with permission of
Gareth Boden

Our thanks to Dr Roger Thetford of the Thames Valley
Orienteering Club for his comments in the preparation of
this book.

Every effort has been made to contact copyright holders
of any material reproduced in this book. Any omissions
will be rectified in subsequent printings if notice is given
to the Publisher.

Any words appearing in the text in bold, **like this**, are
explained in the Glossary.

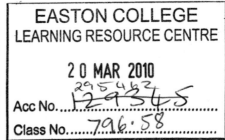

CONTENTS

A MIND AND BODY SPORT

What is orienteering?

Orienteering is a sport in which **competitors** run around a course, finding their way from one **control point** to another using a map and **compass**. The course can vary in length from 2 to 15 kilometres. There are courses for all levels of ability and fitness, from beginners to experienced orienteers, so it's a sport that appeals to people of all ages, from eight to over eighty. It takes place in the fresh air, in wooded countryside, the mountains and on moorland, and combines physical exercise with the mental challenge of **navigation**.

A short history

Orienteering started in Sweden in about 1910. The first official event was held in 1918 and the sport quickly grew to become a major recreational pastime in **Scandinavia**. From there, interest spread far and wide across the world. It was introduced into Britain in the 1960s. The British Orienteering Federation (BOF) was set up in 1967 and there are now about 150 permanent orienteering courses in the British Isles. All are specially designed for newcomers to the sport.

These young orienteers are navigating between control points, using their maps and compasses. They are going as fast as they can, but at the same time making sure they don't go the wrong way!

The rules

At an organized orienteering event competitors set off at one-minute intervals. This means that each competitor is on his or her own, and the winner is the person with the fastest time. The winnner is not known until everyone has finished and all the times have been looked at.

Each runner has to visit all the controls on the course. On average there will be between six and twenty-five controls. These controls have a unique **code** and a patterned needle punch, which is used to mark the **control card** carried by the runner.

Once all the controls have been visited and the runner's card has all the unique patterns of holes in it from the needle punches, there's a mad dash for the finish!

Checking the map for one last time before setting off at the start of an orienteering competition. Notice the protective clothing and gloves worn by this competitor.

There are different types of orienteering competition, but all involve finding your way around unfamiliar territory using a map which marks out the course.

Cross-country

In this event you have to make your way around a course that is shown on a map. **Control points** are marked by circles which are linked by lines. **Competitors** have to go to them in the correct order, punching their card at each point before going on to the next. The fastest competitor wins. This is the most common type of event, and is used for most major national and international championships.

Score events

In this type of competition there are lots of control points (up to 30) and they can be visited in any order. Controls can be worth a different number of points, with the highest points being at those which are farthest away or hardest to find. The winner is the person who collects the most points in a set time, usually one hour.

Relays

In a relay event teams of three or more runners compete against other teams. The first runners from each team start together on their leg of the course. When they finish, the next leg is completed by another person in their team. The first team to cross the finishing line wins.

Relay orienteering in action. Here the first member of the team is handing over to their team mate.

Mountain orienteering

As the name suggests, this event takes place in the mountains. It covers a long distance and tests the fitness and survival skills of the competitors, as well as their **navigational** ability! An extreme version is the mountain marathon event. Here competitors are out for two days, carrying their tents and food in small packs on their backs.

Mountain orienteering – one of the most physically demanding types there is. This competitor has just arrived at a control point. He is carrying a light rucksack.

OTHER EVENTS

 Other events include night orienteering, mountain bike orienteering, ski orienteering and trail orienteering, which can be done by wheelchair competitors.

GETTING STARTED

Thinking about clothing

Orienteering events take place outside, all year round and in all weather. You need to choose clothes to suit the weather and the environment which could be high mountain, low-level forest or heathland. Light, tough clothing that does not absorb water is the best.

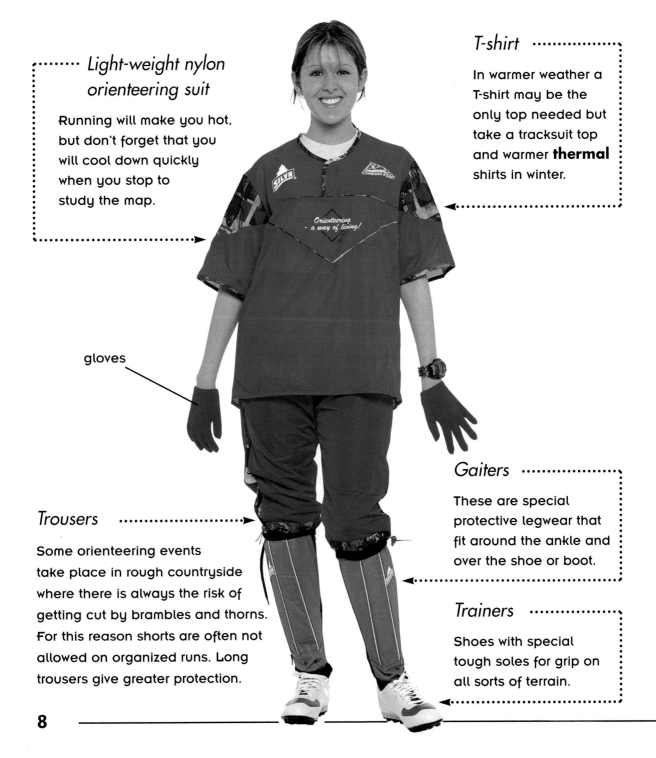

Light-weight nylon orienteering suit

Running will make you hot, but don't forget that you will cool down quickly when you stop to study the map.

T-shirt

In warmer weather a T-shirt may be the only top needed but take a tracksuit top and warmer **thermal** shirts in winter.

gloves

Trousers

Some orienteering events take place in rough countryside where there is always the risk of getting cut by brambles and thorns. For this reason shorts are often not allowed on organized runs. Long trousers give greater protection.

Gaiters

These are special protective legwear that fit around the ankle and over the shoe or boot.

Trainers

Shoes with special tough soles for grip on all sorts of terrain.

Special equipment

Other equipment that you will need includes:

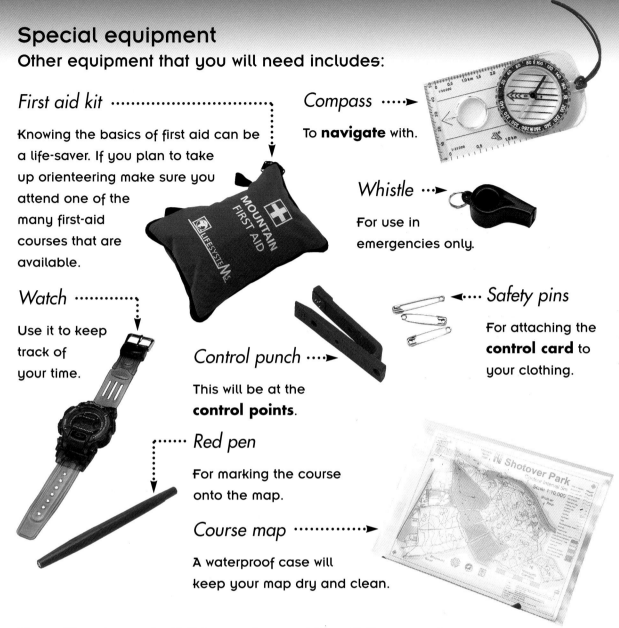

First aid kit ·····························

Knowing the basics of first aid can be a life-saver. If you plan to take up orienteering make sure you attend one of the many first-aid courses that are available.

Compass ·····▶

To **navigate** with.

Whistle ···▶

For use in emergencies only.

Watch ·············

Use it to keep track of your time.

Safety pins ◀····

For attaching the **control card** to your clothing.

Control punch ····▶

This will be at the **control points**.

Red pen

For marking the course onto the map.

Course map ··············▶

A waterproof case will keep your map dry and clean.

You will not need all this equipment for all the events.

SAFETY FIRST

🥾 The wildlife in certain areas and countries can be hazardous, for example poisonous snakes and spiders. Before setting off find out what hazards there are likely to be.

🥾 All the time you run along you must be aware of the ground under your feet. When it becomes very uneven, slow down and pick your way carefully over the pitfalls to avoid injury.

TRAINING

How fit do you need to be?
You don't need to be super-fit to take part in orienteering. When you first start, you may only be able to run for part of the course, and have to walk round the rest. This probably means that you will not win anything – yet! However, simply getting out and taking part will improve your fitness, and work your **cardiovascular system** and muscles. The more ambitious you become, the fitter you will need to be, but don't attempt to run too far or too often. Your body needs time to recover, whatever your fitness level.

Warming up
Get into the habit of warming up before an event or training session and warming down afterwards. Doing this will help your muscles recover, so that you are less stiff the next day.

Warming up should take the form of on-the-spot jogging or skipping. This will increase your heart rate and breathing, warm the muscles up and prepare them for the hard work that lies ahead. On an average orienteering course you will be on the move for between 45 and 90 minutes.

Stretching

Along with warming up, do some stretching before and after orienteering. Hard running tends to stiffen and shorten the **muscle fibres**, which is not good for them. Stretching will help prevent this. Be gentle when stretching – never bounce or make jerky movements.

Adductor and glute stretch ········

Bend your knee and bring it up high. Hold on to it for 10 seconds then swap legs.

Quadricep stretch ············

Bend one knee and pull your foot up behind you. Hold for 10 seconds then swap legs.

Inner thigh stretch ··········

Stand with your feet wide apart, toes facing forward. Bend your front knee and lean forward. Hold the stretch for 10 seconds then do the other leg.

Improving your skills

It is important that you practise running with the map and **compass**. Fitness alone will not make you a better orienteer. You need to work on your technical ability, which means reading the map while running through forests, undergrowth or across moorland.

THE MAP

Reading the map

The map is the most important tool orienteers have to help them **navigate**. Orienteers around the world use specially drawn maps for their events. The **symbols** on them have been standardized. Once you have learnt what they mean, you will be able to interpret any orienteering map.

Scale

The first thing to understand is the **scale** of the map you are using. The most common scales are 1:10,000 or 1:15,000. Beginners sometimes use a larger scale, 1:5,000. You must also check the line on the map that shows **magnetic north**. This will be useful when you set the map using a **compass**.

Setting the map

It is important that you hold the map in the direction you are facing. This is called setting the map. You can do this by lining up features on the ground with those on your map. You can also use the compass, turning the map until the north-south line aligns with that of the north-south direction of your compass needle.

Control Description	1 Path junction	2 Path	3 Northeastern path junction	5 Re-entrant	6 Stream	7 Re-entrant	8 Path	9 Path junction	10 Path junction	11 Earthbank & path crossing	12 Path	13 Marsh (southeast side)	14 Path bend	15 Spur	16 Fence	17 Path	18 Earthbank	19 Stream and path crossing	20 Path junction	21 Fence corner

A typical orienteering map, showing the scale, **contours**, different types of vegetation, paths and where all the control points are to be found.

When the map is set, you should be able to look around you and recognize the features in the landscape on your map. Next you must copy the locations of the **control points** from the **master map** onto your map. Now you're ready to set off!

THE SYMBOLS

- Black symbols – mainly man-made features (roads, paths, fences, walls, power lines, railways lines, buildings). They also show rocky ground.

- Blue symbols – watery features (lakes, rivers, streams, marshes).

- Brown symbols – **contour lines**, which show the shape of the land.

- Green symbols – **vegetation**. Darker green means denser vegetation.

- Yellow symbols – open land (bright yellow indicates fields or grassland and pale yellow shows moorland).

- White – general woodland. You have to look at the green patches within the white to see how thick this is.

Thumbing the map

When you are looking for the next control point, you will need to look frequently at your map. If you stop each time you do this, you will lose precious time. By placing your thumb on the point where you are on the map, you should be able to keep running, checking your position as you go. You will need to move your thumb as your position changes. This is not an easy technique to use, but practice will make you more proficient.

Keep track of where you are on the map while running by putting your thumb on the spot. This competitor is using a red mark on her thumbnail to be super accurate.

Setting the map. Do this by looking at the landscape and lining up the features you see with the features on the map.

THe COMPASS

An important tool

Along with the map, the **compass** is an important tool for **navigation**. The red end of the needle in the compass always points to **magnetic north**. By using the **direction-of-travel arrow** you will always know which way you are facing. This is extremely useful when the landscape is flat and featureless. In this situation, although the map may not help very much in finding the next **control point**, the compass can be relied upon to point you in the right direction – provided you know how to use it correctly!

Setting the map

You can set the map using a compass. To do this, simply turn the map so that its magnetic north lines follow the same direction as the needle on the compass. Once this has been done, all the features you see around you should correspond to those on the map. This is a very useful technique when there are few features to see, or if you are lost. In poor weather conditions you might not be able to see a stream or hill that is only 10 metres away!

Setting the map using the compass. The top of the map points to magnetic north. This should be lined up with the magnetic needle (the red end!) on your compass.

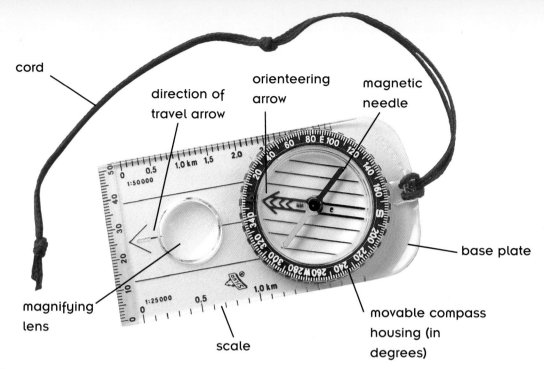

cord

direction of travel arrow

orienteering arrow

magnetic needle

base plate

magnifying lens

scale

movable compass housing (in degrees)

Taking a bearing

Taking a **bearing** means drawing an imaginary line between you and the thing you are trying to get to, such as a control point, fence or stream. The 360-degree circle around the compass needle can then be read to give the actual bearing that you must travel along to get to where you want.

Turn the **compass housing** to line up the direction-of-travel arrow with the direction you want to go in. Keep looking at the compass as you run along the course. Accuracy in reading the compass is essential here. A few degrees out may mean missing your control point.

Choosing a route

When you go on an orienteering event, you will probably not have seen the course before. You will be given time to look at the **master map** and copy down the **control points** onto your own map. You then have to choose the best route to go to each control point. On easy courses there may not be much of a choice – it might be obvious that if you follow a fence you will eventually arrive at a control point.

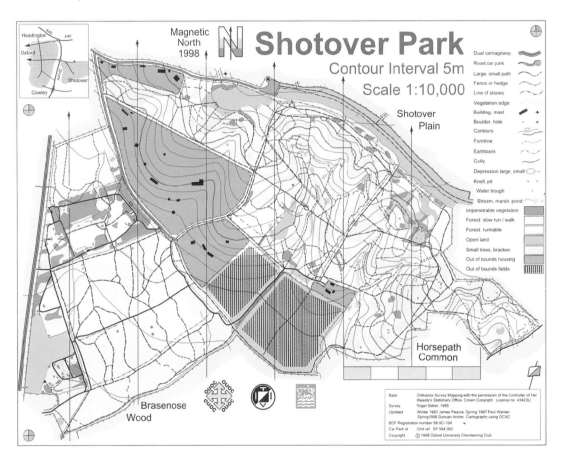

As you progress onto harder courses this will not be the case. You will have to decide whether to go over a hill and down the other side, or around it, and whether to cut directly through a dense forest or go round it. In other words, you must decide whether to take risky short cuts (relying on your skills with a **compass** and map) or safer, longer routes. The choice is yours!

Close study of the map before you set off is vital. If you choose a wrong route between control points, you will lose valuable time.

Using handrails

The safest and fastest way to get to a control point is to follow a **line feature** – if you are lucky enough to have one. These include fences, streams, paths and walls. They are quick to find on the map and once found can easily be followed. They are used as a **handrail**. They may lead you directly to your control, or they may lead you part of the way. You may have to leave the handrail and follow a **bearing** to finish off. Line features are also used for **aiming off**.

Using a handrail is one of the fastest methods of navigating. Here the competitor is using a dried-up stream. He will have memorized the point at which he should leave it to get to his control point.

Attack points

An attack point is an obvious feature, usually found on a handrail, such as the corner where a wall changes direction, or a **stream junction**. An attack point is useful because you should be able to run to it quickly, without having to worry too much about the compass and map. Once you arrive at your attack point you should slow down or even stop to take a bearing on the control point, which might be in the middle of a featureless moor or field.

Estimating distance

Experienced orienteers know how many double paces they take to run 100 metres. With experience they can also begin to judge how far away things are. These techniques make it easier to find difficult **control points**. Used alongside accurate map and **compass** work, estimating distances will help you find even the most difficult control point. But being good at judging distance and knowing how far you have run takes a lot of practice.

Pacing

To work out how many double paces you take to cover 100 metres, find a straight path and measure out 100 metres accurately. Now run along the path, counting every other footfall – if you start on your right foot, only count the pace every time your right foot touches the ground. This is a double pace. Do this several times at your average running speed. Now repeat this, walking at a comfortable pace. Record your running and walking paces for 100 metres and memorize them. You will now have one more technique to fall back on when **navigating** a tricky section of the course.

Pacing is an accurate method of measuring relatively small distances. It can be used when you need to home in on the control point.

Visualization

By looking at features and **contour lines** on the map, you can build up a mental picture of the landscape around a control point. This should help you know when you have arrived in the area close to the control.

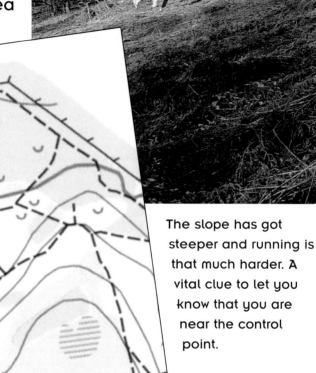

The slope has got steeper and running is that much harder. A vital clue to let you know that you are near the control point.

By careful reading of the map, noting that the contour lines have got closer together, you will have anticipated that steep slope angle and be ready to slow down to home in on your target.

TOP TIP

If you know the **scale** of the map you are using, you can work out the distances between things. Once you have done this, you can work out how many paces you need to get from one place to another. For example, if you know that the corner of a forest is 250 metres away from a rock outcrop you want to get to, and know that you run 100 metres in 44 paces, you can work out that it will take you 110 double paces (2.5 times 44 = 110) to get from the forest to the rock.

GETTING LOST!

Keeping cool

Every orienteer gets lost, even the most experienced. When lost it is important to **relocate** yourself quickly. The most important thing to do is keep calm. It is wise to have a flexible plan already in your head as to what you might do if you get lost. Your plan will then have to be altered according to how lost you think you are and whether or not you are close to the **control point** you're looking for.

How to relocate yourself

If you have been running on a **compass bearing** in a straight line, but can no longer recognize the features around you on the map, the best plan is to trust your compass and keep on the bearing. You may want to slow your pace down and look out for obvious features that may appear, and then find them on the map.

Getting lost is no fun! But stay cool and think about the terrain you have just come through. Look for an obvious landscape feature to help relocate yourself.

If you have been following a more complicated route, then slow down or stop altogether to consider where you might be. Look around for distinctive features that you can then find on your map. You may need to re-set the map with your compass. This should help you to notice details around you. If you still cannot pin-point your position on the map, think back to the last control point. Could you have set off from there 180 degrees in the wrong direction (a fairly common mistake)? If you think this is possible, look at the map and see what the landscape should look like in this new position. Does it fit the actual landscape you see around you?

It is important not to rush relocation. You could end up in a far worse position.

THE EMERGENCY SIGNAL

If there is an accident or you get so lost that you have no idea where you are, you will need to call for help. There is a standard signal that orienteers use: six quick blasts on the whistle at one-minute intervals. Keep doing this until you hear the reply of three blasts on a whistle, which means help is on its way.

Running

Experienced orienteers know that one of the hardest things to do is judge how fast to run. There is an important balance to be struck between keeping up your speed (to win a race) and keeping in contact with the map and **compass** (to avoid getting lost). Most mistakes in orienteering are made through not slowing down enough to check the map and compass. Only you can decide what is too fast. The more experienced you become, the longer you will be able to go without consulting the map and without getting lost as well.

Striking the balance between fast running and keeping a track of where you are on the map is one of the key skills in orienteering.

READING THE MAP ON THE MOVE

This is not an easy skill to learn. It needs a lot of practice. Once mastered, it means that you will be able to **navigate** while running. Here are some useful tips:

- 👟 Always keep your thumb on the part of the map where you are, and move your thumb as your position changes.

- 👟 Keep your map folded small so that it does not flap about.

- 👟 Keep your map in your hand in front of you – don't swing your map arm backwards and forwards.

- 👟 Keep looking briefly at the map when the navigating becomes complicated – but don't fall over a rock or bump into a tree!

If the route gets really tricky, slow right down or start to walk.

Developing your style

By now you will have realized that there are lots of ingredients in orienteering. Orienteers develop different styles. Some concentrate on speed and fitness, others on map work, while a few might be better at compass **bearings** or pacing distances. Whatever you feel your strong points are, don't forget the whole picture. You need to be reasonably good at all these things to succeed in the sport, and perhaps very good at one or two aspects. This will give you your own special style. Don't forget, when the going gets tough, you will fall back on your strengths.

What to expect

Competitions are very exciting to take part in. They will challenge your fitness, speed and **navigational** skills. When you arrive at an event, there may be several different courses on offer, ranging from easy to hard. They may be colour coded. Choose which one you want to enter and then go to the registration area. Once you have opted for a start time, you will be ready to go.

Preparation

It will help if you have warmed up and stretched before you start. Make sure you allow time for this. You will also need time to write your name on your **control card** and copy out the **codes** of each **control point**. You will need a red pen to take down information from the **master map** onto your map.

Take time to copy accurately all the information you will need from the master map onto the map you will carry with you on the course.

It is important that you think about how you are going to carry your map, **compass** and control card. You wil need to get hold of them quickly when on the run. Most orienteers pin the control card to their clothing or tie it around their wrist. Fold the map to a manageable size and carry it in your hand. Keep your compass ready in the other hand.

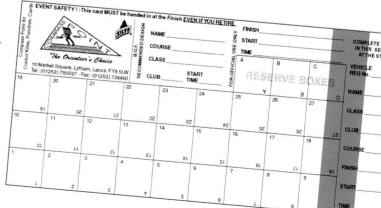

A typical control card. In a competition, you will need to fill in your details on this control card before you set off on the course.

Control points

Control points are usually marked with a red and white triangle. They will have a code, which should be the same as the one on your control card. Take the needle punch that you find there and use it to mark the square on your card next to the correct code.

The finish

You must hand in your control card once you have finished. You must do this even if you have not completed the course. The organizers of the event check the control cards to be sure that everyone has returned safely.

At last – the control point you have been aiming for! Don't forget to record your visit on your card using the needle punch.

COLOUR-CODED EVENTS

- White 1–1.5 km, the easiest course.

- Yellow 1–2.5 km, slightly harder to find some of the control points.

- Orange 2–3.5 km, sometimes there will be a choice of route between the control points.

- Red 4–6 km, longer distances between control points and more choices of route.

- Green, blue and brown courses are of the highest technical difficulty, combined with long distances. These are mainly for experienced orienteers.

HOW TO PLAN A COURSE

Who is the course for?

Anyone can make an orienteering course, provided they understand the principles behind the sport and the practicalities of finding a suitable place to do it. Many clubs run sessions on how to plan a course. First of all you have to know what standard of course you are making. This will effect how long it is and how hard and what features there need to be. Most beginners will enjoy a course at about the yellow standard (see page 25).

If you attempt to plan an orienteering course, don't forget to consider the age and the abilities of the people you are planning it for.

The course

You will need to find some safe public land where you can plan a course that is about 2 kilometres long. Because the course is for beginners, you will need plenty of **line features** to help them. There should be between six and eight **control points** for them to find, with no choices of route to confuse the **competitors**. Make it easy so that they do not have to use a **compass**. They will need a map though. Ask your local club if they have a simple map of the area. If they haven't you will have to make one. You should check that your course can be completed in about 30 minutes. So try it out before you let others loose on it!

Orienteering courses can be planned with all sorts of people in mind. Here a bunch of youngsters and a toddler (under mum's watchful eye) get to grips with the map.

REMEMBER

 Always check that the land you plan to use is not private or that you should not use it for some reason.

Making a map

Your map should use a **scale** of 1:10,000 or 1: 15,000. Make sure you clearly show all line features, such as paths, fences, walls and streams. Clearly mark the start and finish areas. Make sure that your control points are easy to find.

ORIENTEERING FOR ALL

A sport for all ages

People of all ages take part in orienteering. The International Orienteering Federation (IOF) has categories of events that are divided up according to age. These range from events for 10-year-olds to the over-90s!

Once a race has started, the competitors are challenged by the landscape and the difficulties of finding the **control points**. They need their **navigation** skills. If someone is less fit than someone else, they may make up for this by making better route choices or through their more advanced map and **compass** work. Orienteering is much more than simply running in the open air, which is why it appeals to so many people.

Age is no barrier in this sport. You work to your abilities and fitness level, and then decide how far you want to go!

Orienteering for the disabled

There are events designed with the disabled competitor in mind. They are called trail orienteering (or Trail-O for short). Wheelchair competitors move around on level tracks with good surfaces through the countryside to find their control points. All the usual navigational skills are required for the course.

FIND OUT MORE

 To find out more about the types of courses found in your area or throughout the world, you can contact organizations such as the British Orienteering Federation (BOF) or the Orienteering Federation of Australia. They will put you in contact with a local club and also provide a list of permanent courses that can be used by anyone at any time.

Wheelchair competitors take on all the challenges of the sport – fitness, navigational skills, and maybe even a competitive streak!

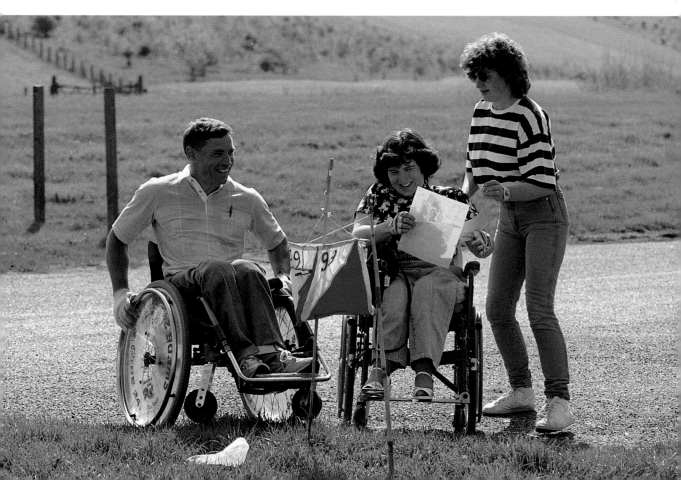

GLOSSARY

aiming off a navigational technique used when you want to check that you turn the correct way when you hit a line feature or handrail

bearing the line of travel or direction that you want to take. A compass bearing is a reading taken from the compass

cardiovascular system the heart and blood vessels that carry oxygen and energy to our muscles

code each control point has a code (either numbers or letters) that no other control point on the course will have

compass a tool for navigation. It has a magnetic needle floating inside a special casing; the red end always points to magnetic north. Another arrow (the direction-of-travel arrow) can be moved around to point to the bearing along which you want to go

compass housing the special casing in which the magnetic needle is set

competitors people who take part in an orienteering event

contour lines lines found on maps that link ground of the same height above sea level

control card a card carried by each competitor. All the control points with their codes will be marked on the card. Competitors punch the card with the needle punch found at each control point to prove they have been there

control point a point on a course, marked by a red and white triangle, with code and needle punch. Each control point is shown on the map as a 5 mm circle

direction-of-travel arrow the moveable arrow found on the base plate of a compass, used to show a bearing

handrail a long feature, such as a river or fence, that can be followed quickly and with confidence to get to a point on the map

line feature a long feature found on a map. If used to help navigation it is called a handrail. Such features include paths, roads, fences, walls and streams

magnetic north the point in the far north of the Earth where all magnets point. The red end of the magnetic needle in a compass points to magnetic north; the lines on an orienteering map also point to magnetic north

master map the map provided by the organizers of an orienteering competition showing all the features and control points

muscle fibres the millions of long, thread-like fibres that make up our muscles

navigating finding your way across an unknown area of land using such tools as a compass and map

relocate the skill of finding where you are if lost

scale the means by which a large area of land can be shown on a small map, for example, at a scale of 1:10,000, 1 centimetre on the map represents 100 metres on the ground

Scandinavia the countries of Sweden, Norway and Denmark

stream junction the point at which two or more streams meet

symbols special shapes or colours used on maps to represent landscape features. For example, a blue line may represent a river, a circle a control point and a black cross a first aid point

thermal materials that trap heat, often used to make warm clothes

vegetation any or all of the plants in a certain area

USEFUL ADDRESSES

British Orienteering Federation
Riversdale
Dale Road North
Darley Dale
Matlock
Derbyshire
DE4 2HX
01629 734042

Ultrasport
The Orienteers' Shop
The Square
Newport
Shropshire
TF10 7AG

Silva (UK) Ltd
PO Box 15
Feltham
Middlesex
TW13 6BD

(for compasses and orienteering equipment)

Suunto
Viking Optical Ltd
Blyth Road
Halesworth
Suffolk
IP19 8EN

(for compasses)

Harvey Maps
12-16 Main Street
Doune
Perthshire
FK16 6BJ

(for maps)

FURTHER READING

Orienteering: The skills of the game,
Carol McNeill, Crowood Press

Orienteering for the Young,
Tom Renfew, Carol McNeill and Peter Palmer, British Orienteering Federation

Orienteering in the National Curriculum,
Peter Palmer and Carol McNeill, British Orienteering Federation

Orienteering, John Disley, Faber

Mapmaking for Orienteers,
Robin Harvey, British Orienteering Federation

Magazines

CompassSport, bimonthly UK magazine

Websites

www.cix.co.uk/~bof/
British Orienteering Federation

INDEX